Shopping: Then and Now

by Cameron Macintosh

OXFORD
UNIVERSITY PRESS
AUSTRALIA & NEW ZEALAND

T0362663

Shopping

Today, we need to shop for many things. We shop for food to eat, clothes to wear and other items that we need for school or work.

A modern shopping centre has lots of different shops.

The way we shop and the things we can shop for have changed over the years. Now, we can buy many things that people couldn't buy in the past. Modern shopping centres sell just about anything we could ever need. We can now shop from the comfort of our own homes, too.

We can now shop at home, using a computer or phone.

Today, we can usually find everything we need in one place.

Did you know?
The world's biggest shopping mall is about the size of 50 sports fields. It has more than a thousand shops!

In the past, people had to go to lots of different small shops to buy everything they needed. Each shop sold one thing, such as bread, shoes or toys. Sometimes the shops were far apart, so it could take people a long time to buy what they needed.

People bought shoes from specialist shoe shops, not **department stores**.

Shopping for Food

Then

In the past, people bought fresh foods that were in season, such as strawberries in summer and parsnips in winter. They bought food grown or made near where they lived. Most foods would **spoil** in the time it took to move them to distant places, as there were no fridges.

People bought food from small shops such as a **greengrocer's**.

Some people grew and made their own food at home, so they did not need to buy as much from shops. They grew fruit and vegetables and baked their own bread and cakes. They didn't have take-away food either.

Supermarkets made food shopping quicker and easier for most people.

Over time, supermarkets and shopping centres began to open. For the first time, people could get everything they needed in one place.

Did you know?
The first supermarket opened about a hundred years ago.

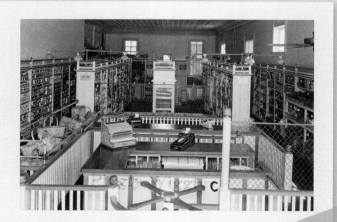

Now

Today, we can buy foods from all around the world. Food can be moved from one place to another on container ships, trucks or aeroplanes. It can be refrigerated so it stays fresh while it's moved from place to place.

Container ships can move large amounts of foods around the world.

Foods that were once thought of as **exotic**, such as herbs, spices and fruits like bananas, can now be bought in most places.

All sorts of herbs and spices are sold in supermarkets.

'**Fast foods**' that are not made at home can be bought from shops. We can also buy frozen and tinned foods that last a long time.

Shopping for Clothes

Then

In the past, most people bought their clothes from small shops or tailors. Their clothes were 'made to measure'. Many people also bought material and thread so they could make their own clothes.

A tailor made sure that clothes fitted perfectly.

Clothes and shoes were made to last a long time. People would mend their clothes if they tore or wore out.

Many people knew how to mend their own clothes.

Children passed their clothes to younger brothers or sisters when they grew too big for them.

Now

Today, we can go to shopping centres to buy everything we need to wear. In one trip, we can buy shoes, shirts, trousers or dresses.

We can compare the prices of items at different shops in the same shopping centre.

We can now buy clothes from home, online. We can pay online and have the clothes delivered. Many of the clothes we buy online are made overseas and shipped around the world.

Before buying online, we need to search for the particular item we want and find the right size.

Shopping for Home Goods

Then

In the past, items for the home were sold in small shops. People went to these shops to buy items for their kitchens, living rooms and bedrooms.

Powered goods such as televisions, fans and toasters were sold in special shops, too.

At first, very few people could afford to buy televisions.

Did you know?
The first televisions were sold in shops about 80 years ago.

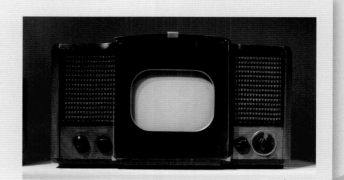

Now

Today, big shops sell a wide range of powered goods. With the rise of **mass production** in factories, goods like televisions and washing machines have become cheaper. They are made in large numbers and shipped around the world.

Many people buy these items online. Online shops keep their goods in huge buildings called warehouses. When you order an item, the seller sends it from the warehouse to your home.

Many workers are needed to run a huge warehouse like this one.

Shopping for Toys

Then

In the past, most people bought toys from small toy shops. Many toys were made by hand, using wood or fabric. People looked after their toys carefully and did not buy as many of them.

Handmade toys lasted a long time if they were well looked after.

Now

Today, we can buy all sorts of toys that people could not buy in the past. These include lots of small toys, made of plastic. Many toys are now powered. They need to be charged before they will work.

Electronic toys are popular to buy.

Did you know?

This small cube, called the Rubik's Cube, is the bestselling toy of all time! More than 350 million have been sold around the world.

Changing Ways to Pay

The way we can pay for our shopping has changed over time. In the past, customers paid shopkeepers with cash — coins or notes. We can still pay for goods with cash today, but we can also pay in other ways.

Many children liked to buy sweets at the milk bar.

Did you know?
Coins were first used by Greek people, more than 2000 years ago.

Cards let us pay for goods without using cash. When the card is tapped on a special machine, the shop receives money from the customer's bank account.

In the past, people could pay a **deposit** for an item, and then small amounts over time. Then they could pick up the item when the payments were complete. Today we can use a credit card – we borrow money from the bank to pay for an item, take it home, and repay the bank later on.

Today, we use barcodes instead of price tags to find out how much something costs.

Old is New

Today, old ways of shopping are becoming popular again. More people want to buy fresh foods from the farmers who grow them. In many places, farmers markets draw large crowds of people each week.

At farmers markets, shoppers can get to know the people who grow and make their foods.

Many people also like to buy handmade goods from the people who make them, rather than buying items made in factories from big shops. These goods include artworks, toys and items to give as gifts.

Handmade goods like these can only be bought at small shops or special markets.

Shopping keeps changing!

1700s .... Small, family-run shops

1880s .... First cash register

1890s .... First big variety stores

1930s .... First shopping centre,
first drive-through take-away food store

1940s .... Many people bought fridges for their homes

1970s .... Barcode (technology) invented

1980s .... First cards used instead of cash

2000s .... Online shopping begins

2020s and ... How will people shop in the future?
beyond   What will they buy and how will they pay?

Glossary

department stores: large shops stocking lots of goods in different departments

deposit: money paid to reserve an item

exotic: something unusual that comes from another part of the world

fast foods: foods that can be cooked quickly

greengrocer's: a shop that sells fruit and vegetables

mass production: making large amounts of things

spoil: to go bad or become damaged

Index